working dogs

working dogs

TALES FROM ANIMAL PLANET'S K-9 TO 5 WORLD

COLLEEN NEEDLES
KIT CARLSON

PHOTOGRAPHS BY KIM LEVIN

Discovery Books

NEW YORK

contents

48 CUSTOMS INSPECTOR
Goldie ❖ Jamaica Plains, N.Y.

52 TV STAR
Wesley ❖ White Plains, N.Y.

56 STATE TROOPER
Xena ❖ Oakdale, Minn.

58 PHYSICAL THERAPISTS
Susie and Thor ❖ White Bear Lake, Minn.

62 GROUNDSKEEPER
Tattie ❖ Hudson, Ohio

64 ARSON DETECTIVE
Lucy ❖ Marblehead, Mass.

68 FOOD TASTERS
Sarah, Joe, Dottie, and Claire ❖ Kansas City, Mo.

72 TELEVISION ICON
Lassie ❖ Canyon City, Calif.

74 CHAPLAIN
Scruffy ❖ Salt Lake City, Utah

78 POLITICAL CONSULTANT
The Bulldog Formerly Known as Franklin ❖ St. Paul, Minn.

82 HOMELESS ADVOCATE
Ginny ❖ Long Beach, N.Y.

84 FARMHAND
Belle ❖ Courtland, Minn.

88 ADVERTISING SPOKESPERSON
Gidget ❖ Irvine, Calif.

90 BOWLING PIN CHASER
Bosco ❖ Homosassa Springs, Fla.

sammy ROOFER

Up the ladder. Down the ladder. Fetch the hammer. Get the pouch loaded with nails. Up the ladder again. This has been the rhythm of Sammy's life since he was a pup. He was born to it, you might say: Chuck Stevens, his owner, was laying a roof for a family whose yellow lab had just had puppies. When Stevens offered to trade work on their chimney for a pup, Sammy became his.

By the time he was four months old, Sammy was bored. Ducks from a nearby pond would come to perch on the family's swing set, so Sammy started chasing them. Soon, he was catching them, and Stevens' wife, Leanne, drew the line. "I can't deal with dead ducks all over my yard," she said. "You've got to take him to work with you."

But Sammy was still looking for a way to occupy himself. He found it one day when one of the men on Stevens' crew hit his thumb with a hammer. The man yelled, throwing his hammer off the roof and into the nearby woods. In a flash, Sammy went after it, and proudly carried the tool back up the ladder to him.

Now Sammy helps on every job. He's a celebrity of sorts in Pembroke, Massachusetts, well known and welcome at every lumber yard and hardware store. And even when he's off-duty, Sammy stays true to his trade. For his toy, no common Frisbee will do—Sammy chases the lid from a bucket of joint compound.

◦ 7 ◦

Not just an important member of the construction team, Sammy's also a hit with the home owners, who give him doggie treats throughout the day.

After a long, hard shift at work, the celebrated lab looks forward to his second job: playmate to the Stevens' four young kids.

karli SCOUT MASTER

several times each summer, a church youth camp in Gregory, Michigan, finds campers earning merit badges, taking hikes, and having fun. The only difference is that this is a Dog Scouts of America camp, and it's chiefly for canines. Some forty people and their dogs have come to learn new skills to do together, including water safety and rescue procedures.

Dog Scout camp could not happen without Karli, an energetic border collie who serves as a counselor for camp director Lonnie Olson. Karli demonstrates how dogs can carry life vests to drowning people. She helps campers earn their backpacking badges by modeling the proper way to carry a pack. She's adept at demonstrating the intricacies of the obstacle course. And she'll even don one of the camp's special sponge-painting booties to create a picture during arts and crafts hour. But she's first and foremost a water baby: If she even so much as hears the sound of someone else splashing in the lake, "she's shaking, just beside herself from wanting to dive in," says Olson. This passion actually proved to be a stumbling block while earning her own lifesaving badge: She struggled to "honor" other dogs, to stay on shore while they took their turn in the lake.

On the last night of Dog Scout camp, everyone gathers around the campfire to share the week's triumphs and sing. Then, before turning in, Karli and Olson lead one last group howl. The voices—hound and human—rise with the wood smoke until the forest rings with the sound.

⚬ 11 ⚬

Karli (flanked by two of her trainees, *above*) has instructed canine campers from as far away as Japan and Denmark.

batty MODEL

Sitting quietly on a high wooden stool, Batty waits to be dressed for the next photo shoot. She gazes about peacefully as a stylist fastens a long, flowered dress around her neck. She holds her head erect as a curly blond wig is flipped over her ears. Then another photographer's assistant slides up under the dress and gently hugs Batty from behind, slipping human hands out through the sleeves.

Batty doesn't mind the costume, the wig, the arms circling her soft, gray flanks. She doesn't mind the bright lights of the Manhattan studio, the chattering people, the snapping camera. She listens closely as her master—the artist William Wegman—talks her through the shoot. Wearing human clothes, posing in strange positions, waiting for a word of direction, are all in a day's work for the weimaraner. She was born to be an artist's model.

Batty is the daughter of Fay Ray, Wegman's second weimaraner, the dog that really came to dominate his art in the 1980s and early '90s. Wegman had often filmed and photographed his first weimaraner, Man Ray, but he hesitated to continue that work with Fay. "I didn't photograph Fay for six months until I realized she was waiting for something to do," he explains. "She knew it was something special."

Batty, on the other hand, has been posing since she was a puppy, and she takes the work in stride. "Fay was marvelous and strong," Wegman says, "but Batty is sweet and easy. Batty can lie very still while I

● 13 ●

completely bury her in objects. I can just put her up there and let her mind wander around ... she will give me a whole lively range of expressions."

It's a quality that makes Batty a perfect Cinderella or Little Red Riding Hood in Wegman's children's books, or an amusing chef or whistling weimaraner in his Alphabet Soup video. Batty and three other dogs—her son Chip, her brother Chundo, and her sister Crooky—form a sort of acting/modeling troupe for Wegman. They've appeared in short videos on *Sesame Street*, played parts in several picture books, and also posed for surrealistic photographs that have hung in art galleries around the world.

And although they spend 90 percent of their time just being ordinary pets, the weimaraners understand themselves to be dogs with a purpose. Each dog enjoys being chosen to be the subject of a photograph. If one of them is working in a

different room, the others get agitated and want to join in. "They come at it with the attitude of, 'What are we going to work on today?'" Wegman says. "In fact, if I'm [just] painting, Batty will come in and look around and get frustrated. It's almost as if she says, 'What do you want me to do? I know you're working on something.'"

After skillful prepping by Wegman (*p. 12*), Batty morphs into Little Red Riding Hood; Chundo becomes the wolf (*opposite and above*). Batty has been known to fall asleep modeling: Assistants stand by to catch her if she topples mid-snooze.

hunter SEARCH & RESCUE SPECIALIST

Hunter was still fresh from his search-and-rescue training when the call came. The Alfred P. Murrah Federal Building in Oklahoma City had been blown up. There was hope that some people might be alive under the rubble. Could Hunter come? Hunter and his handler, Bruce Speer, left immediately as part of the elite Puget Sound task force of FEMA, the Federal Emergency Management Agency.

"It was very emotional for all of us," Speer recalls. "We had been training for natural disasters, and then this. It was a big difference, because someone had done this on purpose." Fortunately, in a way, Hunter was called off the search. He hadn't been trained to search for dead bodies, only living people, and it was soon clear that no one else would be found alive in the wreckage. Instead, Hunter went on stress patrol. He was available to searchers as they came in from the site, for play, for petting, for a momentary respite from their overwhelming anxieties and sorrows.

When an exhausted Speer and Hunter returned to their home in Seattle, they did cadaver training so they would not be caught unprepared again. The training has paid off in the more than one hundred searches Hunter has made since. Most notably, Hunter helped his team find seven lost bodies in the smoldering ruins of a huge apartment fire.

Speer adopted Hunter as a seven-week-old pup, after searching across the United

taught to climb and balance before he could even start his scent work.

While Hunter was raised for this calling, Speer came to it through personal tragedy. A locksmith by trade, Speer does this volunteer search-and-rescue work on the side, to honor the memory of several friends who died in a canoe accident in 1973. Their bodies were never found. "I want to make sure people don't have the anguish of not having a body to say goodbye to," he explains.

Hunter doesn't know about such pain. He just loves his job, loves the searching, the roaming over rubble, the fierce games of tug-of-war that are his rewards. He is fearless, agile, and focused—so focused that Speer is already planning how he will keep Hunter happy when the shepherd's physical talents begin to fade with age. "I'll have to keep him thinking he has some job to do. He'll be retired, but he won't understand that."

States for just the right canine to train for disaster work. He sought one that seemed driven yet mentally focused, one that would be no larger than eighty pounds at adulthood. He even checked for black toenails, because dogs with this trait purportedly have stronger paw pads.

When Hunter came home, the lessons began immediately. He had to be gentled, acclimated to strange surroundings, and

Bruce Speer and his wife Jacquie play human hide-and-seek (p. 16) as part of Hunter's training. They practice at a recycling center managed by friend Fritz Mack (*above, right* with Jacquie and Bruce). *Right:* Rowdy tug-of-war relaxes Hunter.

simon SINGER/SONGWRITER

On his five-song Christmas CD, *Simon Night*, he growls and moans a fervent "Ave Maria." He yips and zips through "God Rest Ye Merry Gentlemen." And, thanks to dubbed-in sound effects, he even performs a jazz arrangement of "Santa Claus Is Comin' to Town" to a tavern packed with cheering fans. Simon, a seven-year-old golden retriever with a voice that spans three octaves, has a gift some singers can only dream of.

Taking that talent public was easy for Simon's owner, Joe Lenarz. As a programmer for a musical notation software company, Lenarz knew just where to find musicians, arrangers, and a mastering studio. He and Simon laid down all the vocal tracks for the dog's first CD in their living room, using a DAT recorder, a series of simple hand signals to indicate when to bark or growl, and a pile of doggie treats for inspiration.

But like the '60s group The Monkees, or the Spice Girls in their early, over-dubbed days, Simon's skill owes something to the artifice of his producer. While Simon's voice is not manipulated or enhanced, it is edited, so that the right notes sound at the proper place in each song. Because of this, he can't perform live. Still, "Santa Claus Is Comin' to Town," with its rowdy crowd, remains Simon's most popular single, Lenarz says. "It's more fun to believe that Simon's really up on stage in a bar. The appeal is in the mystery, like Santa Claus himself."

Simon sometimes gets his "dog" and "singer" commands mixed up: Because he interprets requests to growl and roll over in the same way, the dog first flops onto his side before warbling a response to Lenarz's cue.

glenda NURSE'S AIDE

Shelli Nelson, the hospital cardiac nurse clinician, and Glenda, the black labrador, enter the room together. Nelson is there to tell the recovering patient how to live life anew after heart surgery. It's not pleasant news—there are a lot of old habits she will have to relinquish, a lot of changes that must be made. So they don't talk about that. They focus on Glenda instead.

Glenda is Nelson's ice-breaker, her companion, her partner, her guide. Because Nelson is blind—perhaps the only blind R.N. in the United States with a nursing job—she needs Glenda to help her get around. But she also needs Glenda to help her do her job. "There might be times when patients aren't ready to deal with what I have to say, so we talk about Glenda first. Then we talk about their pets, and I segue into their trip home and what they're going to have to do." Glenda is her best visual aid, her object lesson. When Nelson tells a patient there can't be any more bacon or hamburgers, it's hard to argue with her. Glenda is living evidence that life can change dramatically and still go on. "I don't tell them my story, but they see me with the changes I've had to incorporate. And they can't then refuse to give up hamburgers," she laughs.

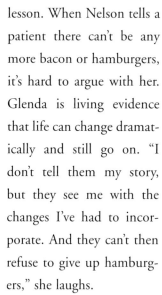

Nelson's juvenile diabetes made her blind in 1985, the same year she graduated from nursing school. When she decided that, blind or no, she still wanted to be a nurse, she had to fight to get licensed in Minnesota. The permit she finally won says she can do any kind of nursing that does

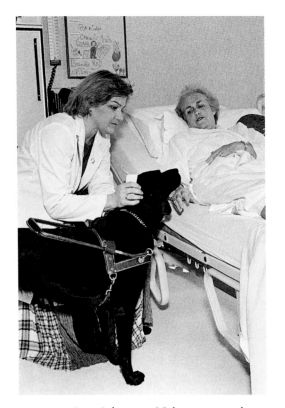

be. "Glenda gives me the confidence I need when I'm standing up lecturing in front of a hundred people. With a cane, I would have less mobility. With a person guiding me, I would become dependent on them. With Glenda, it's teamwork, and people see me differently. They see me not as a blind person, but as someone like them, someone with a dog."

And when Glenda's at home and out of harness, she is just a family pet. She jumps on the bed, chases the cat, and plays tug-of-war with her rope bone. But if Nelson needs her, Glenda's right there, and not another person in the world can distract her. She's all business, taking it seriously, correcting herself if necessary before Nelson even says a word. As far as Glenda is concerned, any job of Nelson's is a job of hers as well.

not require sight, so Nelson created an educational job for herself in the cardiac intensive care unit of Fairview Southdale Hospital in Edina. She leads classes, coaches patients on life after surgery, and teaches pain management.

Without Glenda, however, none of this would be possible. She frees Nelson to be the capable, caring nurse she was trained to

As a guide dog, Glenda makes Shelli Nelson's life manageable; as a special visitor, Glenda lifts a patient's spirits. On this day, she and Nelson spend time with Donald Hammer (p.23) and Lois Belanger (above and right).

tess SECURITY GUARD

Tess raised her head as the pointed black ears of her mother, Cassie, snapped to attention. Just beyond the light of the campfire, there was a rustling in the trees of Montana's Bob Marshall Wilderness. The unmistakable scent of bear floated on the air. The grizzly that had been harassing this hunters' camp was back. In an instant, the dogs were up, barking furiously.

For five hours, the enormous bear circled the campsite. True to her training, veteran dog Cassie kept up an uninterrupted, seemingly effortless stream of barking as the bear paced around the camp. Tess, however, was still young, not yet a champion barker. Trying mightily, she followed her mother's lead and maintained a barrage of noise. Overhead, constellations rose and set,

the moon eased westward, morning approached. In the end, the bear could not outlast these Karelian bear dogs, as this special breed is known. Ears ringing from the onslaught, he slunk off in defeat. The canines had trained another reluctant student, and Tess had admirably earned her bear dog diploma.

Tess belongs to the Utah-based Wind River Bear Institute, which operates a one-of-a-kind "Partners in Life" program to teach both bears and humans how to coexist. Tim Manley, a Montana grizzly bear management specialist, works with the program and takes care of Tess. Like her late mother had been, Tess today is a master of the technique called "bear shepherding," a nonviolent way to deal with bears who find humans and their foodstuffs easy pickings.

27

States, Tess and other Karelian bear dogs could help preserve a threatened species.

Bred first in Finland to hunt bears in the Scandinavian forests, these striking, black-and-white dogs are cool customers. Weighing only about fifty pounds and armed with nothing more than speed, attitude, and bark, Karelians think nothing of facing down a 400-pound animal. In fact, Tess was treeing black bears with the aplomb and efficiency of her mother before she was even a year old.

The stellar performances of Cassie (whose pioneering work launched the program), Tess, and other Karelians have given Hunt, Manley, and other wildlife experts hope that somehow humans and bears might be able to coexist in the shrinking American wilderness. But it can only be done one bear at a time, and these dogs can't be everywhere at once. Fortunately, more and more Karelians are being used in wildlife management, all of whom share with Tess a single desire—to get out into the woods and start teaching some bears some manners.

The method was developed by the Institute's director, bear biologist Carrie Hunt, who uses Karelians to train bears to associate human habitats with the repetitive, loud, irritating barks of stubborn dogs. It is a promising alternative to the more common approach of trapping and relocating or even destroying the ursine intruders. With fewer than a thousand grizzlies left in the lower 48 United

Karelians are all bark, no bite ... just don't tell the bears. Even the wildlife managers pack rubber bullets to kindly drive the point home when necessary. *Previous page, from left:* Tim Manley (with Tess), Rick Yates, Angela Klinefelter.

kersee

Image is everything in public relations, and Kersee, an executive for Iams, the pet food company, is a mistress of image. Sleekly blond, well groomed, and well behaved, Kersee often acts as an official company representative at charity functions, and frequently attends board meetings to provide a dog's perspective on pet food. With a softly waving tail and a white-toothed smile, this amiable golden retriever is the public face of a corporation that might otherwise remain nondescript.

Kersee's day begins at 8 A.M., when she arrives at Iams headquarters in Dayton, Ohio, with her human companion, systems analyst Teresa Pearson. For most of the day, Kersee greets visitors as they enter the lobby, or drops in on employees, looking for pats and dog biscuits. She'll walk in on meetings or stroll through a presentation, but Kersee won't disrupt anything. She has been trained not to beg, jump up, steal food, or sniff anyone in an untoward fashion. She is a perfect lady for forty hours a week.

But when 5 P.M. rolls around, Kersee knows it's quitting time. She heads for Pearson's office and quietly, but insistently, makes her appeal.

Waiting at home are another dog to play with and six acres to roam. There, she can forget the high-stress life of a company executive and just kick back. Like her fellow employees, Kersee is working for the weekend.

Iams employees Kenneth Applin and Mollie Wheeler (*opposite*) meet with P.R. maven Kersee.

amazing mongrels

It's 8 P.M., and the Comedy Barn in Pigeon Forge, Tennessee, explodes with applause as nine barking, bouncing mutts take the stage in a choreographed whirl. They jump rope, roll barrels, climb ladders, walk tight-ropes, steal hats, drop letters into mailboxes, and leap off platforms. Then, for the grand finale, a fluffy dog steps onto a rope held between ringmaster Bob Moore and his assistant. She stands on her hind paws, beautifully balanced.

The crowd cheers and whistles as the Amazing Mongrels charge off stage, barking happily. *Good show! Good show!* they seem to be saying as they nuzzle each other and Moore. The audience was hot tonight—the dogs could feel it—and they flew through the act on the crowd's energy. "They know,"

Moore explains. "They're professional actors. If the audience is a dud, they'll just go through the motions, or else they'll actually get mad and start barking at the people."

Bob Moore is a pro, too—he's been doing this act for years, after picking it up from his father, Dwight, whose Madcap Mutts were the toast of vaudeville in the 1930s. Walt Disney loved the dog troupe and lured them to Hollywood, so Bob Moore grew up on sound-stages and back lots. It was only natural that his Amazing Mongrels would continue the tradition. They've worked in movies, on Broadway, and on television, even jetting off to Chile and Hawaii for special appearances.

Also like his father, Moore rescues all his dogs from animal shelters. He uses a simple test to select his stars: He'll cradle a mutt in his arms on its back, like a baby. If it doesn't squirm, or try to twist away, he knows it trusts him enough to be teachable. He introduces the newcomer to the rest of the dogs and lets pack society have its way. "They realize they were out of their element before, and now they're in a pack the way they're supposed to be," Moore says. "And I'm the top dog, so none of them ever fights."

In this pack, according to Moore, each dog's dominant breed determines its behavior, and thus its role in the act. Spot, the border-collie mix, is the smart one, so she gets to do math by barking. Ginger, who's mostly Norwich terrier, works the crowd at the front of the stage. Skeeter, a collie mix, is the daredevil, the one who walks the high wire and balances on the rope. Some work for treats, some for love, some for the sheer joy of performing. "Spot, for instance, gets insulted if you pay her off with food," Moore notes. "Her work is her life."

Bob Moore's Amazing Mongrels have been honored with numerous awards for their spirited act.

nicky

The Coast Guard cutter pulls up alongside the fishing boat. "This is the Coast Guard. We're coming aboard. There's a canine in our boarding party," the captain yells. Nicky leaps over, dragging his handler, Rusty Merritt, behind. The boarding party begins its safety check, but Nicky doesn't care about precautions. Excited, he knows it's time for his favorite game: "Find! Fetch!" He's trying to detect the scent that means, "Good boy!" Suddenly, he stops and starts scratching wildly at a bulkhead. In an instant, the officers' focus switches from safety to crime. Nicky has given the boarding party probable cause to search for drugs, and when the bulkhead is pulled back, bales of marijuana are found. Nicky has won the game. Now he gets to play tug-of-war.

For Nicky, life is play. The German Shepherd is so obsessed by his toys that when he's let out to do his business, he'll run to his barrel of playthings first. He'll spend hours trying to pick up a basketball with his mouth; he'll drop a tennis ball in a trash can, dig it out, then drop it back in over and over again. When he's loose in the house, he wants to search, search, search until he finds a toy, and then implores the handiest human to play. The Merritt family has to give Nicky at least two hours a day of walks, training, and play to keep him calm enough to live with.

The drive to search and play makes Nicky an outstanding drug detector. But his zeal was almost his undoing. As a growing puppy, Nicky wore out two owners with his relentless energy. When his frazzled second

family gave up and sent him to the pound, no one there wanted him, either. Nicky was just one day from being euthanized when German Shepherd Rescue of New England, Inc., realized his boundless energy could be put to good use, and found him a job with the Coast Guard.

Rusty Merritt, founder of the Coast Guard's canine program, took a chance on the hyperactive dog. They took it slowly at first, just bonding and building trust. Then Merritt acclimated Nicky to new environments, taught him to slog through swamps, to jump from one boat to another, even to ride calmly in a helicopter. Only then was Nicky trained to channel his obsession with playing into the single game of "Find! Fetch!"

Now, Nicky sets the standard for the other dogs Merritt is training for the Coast Guard. But no other canine comes close. When Merritt and Nicky are working together, the dog draws the human into his game. Everything becomes a mystery to be solved, a toy to be found. "After you've trained a dog like Nicky," says Merritt, "any other dog just seems like hard work."

◎ **39** ◎

Usually, just the imposing sight of Nicky storming onto their boat is enough to make guilty parties give up their stash.

uga V CHEERLEADER

Sanford Stadium in Athens, Georgia, was awash in red and black. University of Georgia fans packed the stands, ostensibly to see the Bulldogs face South Carolina. But they were also there to watch Uga V, the team mascot, retire after ten years of service. *"Damn good dog! Damn good dog!"* The stadium rocked with the traditional cry as, midfield, the mascot's spiked collar was removed from Uga V's neck and strapped around that of his son, Uga VI.

It was the end of an era, one filled with glory for Uga V. The mascot came to national attention in 1996, when he lunged at an Auburn receiver who scored a touchdown. Then he made the cover of *Sports Illustrated* in 1998 as best college mascot.

But his real moment of stardom came that same year when he appeared in Clint Eastwood's film *Midnight in the Garden of Good and Evil.* Eastwood had flown in a stand-in bulldog from California in case the real Uga proved uncooperative. But Uga did Georgia proud, and the stand-in was left standing off-camera.

Retirement was hard for Uga V, who would get a bit querulous on game days. His old duffel bag, filled with jersey and treats, would get carried out the door, after which Uga VI would jump into the car. Then it all clicked for V. He'd scratch at the door and whine, almost as though he could hear the chanting: *"Damn good dog! Damn good dog!"* Two months after his last game, Uga V died of heart failure.

41

The father-son handoff from Uga V (*opposite, foreground*) to Uga VI continued a bloodline tradition begun in 1956. The Frank Seiler family has cared for the dogs the whole time. Like all departed Ugas, Uga V earned a stadium-grounds burial.

wheely willy

The squeak of wheels and the clacking of tiny claws on linoleum herald Willy's arrival on the spinal cord injury unit of Long Beach Veteran's Administration Hospital. Up and down the hallways, paraplegic and quadriplegic veterans in wheelchairs and hospital beds stir with excitement. "Hey, Willy's here!" "It's the para-pup!" A four-pound black Chihuahua careens around the corner in a canine cart—a sort of doggie wheelchair—and the atmosphere lightens with his approach. Wheely Willy's here for his monthly visit to the vets.

Willy is one visitor the vets love to see, because he's more than just a cheer-you-up kind of pup. Willy's been there. Willy *is* there. Willy is a paraplegic, too, with a hard-luck story to match their own. Willy was abandoned in a cardboard box on a city street, his back broken below the fourth vertebra, his throat and vocal cords cut. For a year, he languished in a veterinary hospital. He was in no pain, and could be expected to live a normal life span, but no one wanted Willy. One day, Deborah Turner walked into the office and offered to find Willy a family. It wasn't until she brought him home that Turner realized the family should be hers.

Turner was happy to carry Willy around, to fatten him up, to express his bladder every few hours, to find the right kind of therapies to build his strength. But getting him mobile proved more difficult. At one point, Turner even tied helium

● **43** ●

and schools. Now he makes as many as eighteen visits each month.

Despite everything he's endured, Wheely Willy is cheerful, affectionate, trusting, and docile. Because he can't jump around, Willy can safely be put in bed with sick children hooked up to tubes and machines. Because he has suffered a spinal cord injury, the veterans see Willy as someone who, somehow, understands. And because he has rallied from every setback and blow, psychiatric patients realize that if Willy is happy, maybe they can be happy someday, too.

balloons to Willy's waist in an effort to lift his back end so that he could walk on his front paws. When she finally saw an ad for canine carts, she knew she had found the answer: Willy needed wheels.

Customers in Turner's dog grooming salon loved seeing Willy, and their reactions inspired her to launch his motivational career. People wanted to meet Willy, to hear his story. Willy, in turn, wanted to meet people, to be petted, and to show off his speedy turns in the cart. Turner started taking him to hospitals, nursing homes,

After five years of visiting, Turner understands the force of Willy's appeal: "When you're in a situation where all you can say is, 'Now what?', Willy shows you that there can be a 'what,' and that it will be all right."

Veterans James Goodman (*p. 42*) and David Hernandez (*opposite*) find Wheely Willy to be a kindred soul.

wrangler ACTOR

Please don't bother me. I am an actor. I am studying my part. When Wrangler's on the set, his crate bears—with a certain emphasis—this notice. Because people forget. They want to pet him and play with him. But this Australian cattle dog needs to stay focused. He has to be fresh for take after take after take. So Wrangler rests alone, waiting to be called.

Then, when the director says, "Rolling ... action!" Wrangler comes alive, ready and able to do just about anything. Sit, stay, lie down, play dead—piece of cake. Climb a ladder, open drawers, answer the phone, work the computer—no problem. Wrangler can also "drive" a car and lift his back left leg on command. Plus, he can do eight or more of these behaviors in sequence, which allows for long, uninter-

rupted takes. But even this eager actor has his limits. One day, Wrangler had done twenty takes of jumping through a hula hoop, and he was done in. When the director once again yelled, "... Action!" Wrangler looked up with disgust and lifted his back leg.

This impeccable sense of timing won Wrangler supporting roles in two feature films: *Black Dawn* with Lorenzo Lamas (released in Europe and on home video as *Good Cop, Bad Cop*), and *Very Bad Things* with Christian Slater and Cameron Diaz. But Wrangler's still waiting for his big break, for the *Air Bud* or *Homeward Bound* that could catapult him to stardom. In the meantime, he does what aspiring actors all over Hollywood do while they wait to be discovered. He makes commercials.

⊕ **47** ⊕

"We're like the Lone Ranger and Tonto, but I don't know who's who," owner Don McDaniel says of his buddy Wrangler.

goldie CUSTOMS INSPECTOR

After a long, grueling flight from Europe, arriving passengers at JFK International Airport in New York are delighted to be welcomed by a friendly face. Goldie the beagle waits in the baggage claim area to greet the newcomers, panting happily. People swarm around, patting him and talking silly. But as the baggage carousel revs up and people start collecting their luggage, some of those folks suddenly discover why there's a dog at the baggage claim. Goldie wanders around at the end of a long leash, sniffing the suitcases as they come off the line. Sometimes, he sits right next to a bag. *Busted.*

Goldie's handler, plant protection and quarantine officer Jim Armstrong, approaches. The bag's owner looks down at Goldie, so dashing in a little green coat that says, "Protecting American Agriculture," and asks, "What a cute little dog! Why is he sitting next to my bag?" Armstrong says, "Hi. How are you doing? Do you have any food in your bag today?"

Sometimes, the passenger will apologize profusely and pull out an orange or a forgotten piece of sandwich. But other travelers, those who thought they could sneak pounds of hidden ham or sausage into America, sometimes get belligerent as Armstrong confiscates their foodstuffs and fines them $250 on the spot. Once, an irate passenger even booted Goldie across the baggage claim. Fortunately, there are airport police to take care of such troublemakers: As an officer of the U. S. government, Goldie must suffer no harm.

⊛ 49 ⊛

This beagle is a proud member of the U.S. Department of Agriculture's Beagle Brigade, the first line of defense against food-borne pests and diseases that must be kept off American soil. Even Goldie's name indicates the importance of his job: He's named after the golden nematode, a microscopic insect which destroyed the potato fields that once blanketed Long Island. Goldie and his fellow brigadiers work to halt incursions of hog cholera, swine fever, fruit flies, and any hitchhiking insect or disease that could threaten the nation's agriculture.

Although he lives in a kennel with the rest of the Beagle Brigade (the confusing food smells in a typical home could undermine his abilities), Goldie is, in Armstrong's words, his "baby," his pride and joy, so bonded to his "daddy" that he would work just for love,

although he does appreciate the chewy treats that are his official reward. And he's a champion sniffer. Initially trained to identify five scents—mango, apple, citrus, beef, and pork—Goldie within a year learned to distinguish at least a hundred different odors.

Goldie finds one or two offenders in almost every round of baggage. Sometimes he'll get confused and alert, or call attention, to a fruit-scented perfume or shampoo, but even that kind of mistake has proven useful. Once, a passenger concealed imported ham under a dozen lemon-scented automobile air fresheners, so Goldie alerted to the powerful smell of citrus. *Busted*.

Goldie and handler Jim Armstrong (*p. 48*) take the day's haul of contraband to the "grinder" (*opposite*), where the food and any potential contaminants are destroyed.

wesley TV STAR

"**K**ill me. Go ahead. I'll sit on the floor and you can push the television over on me." The voice here belongs to David Letterman, but it just as easily could be Tim Allen's, or Drew Carey's, or any of the other famous comedians who take turns speaking the thoughts of Wesley, the wrinkled little Brussels griffon who serves as a living sight gag on ABC's hit series *Spin City*. Wesley plays Ronald R. Ragamuffin III—Rags for short—the feeble, thirty-five-year-old pet of New York City mayoral aide Carter Haywood, Michael Boatman's character on the show. Where other television dogs get their laughs from doing tricks, Wesley gets his just by looking as if he has two paws in the grave.

Because he came to acting later in life,

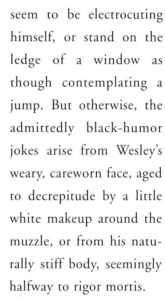

after a career as a show dog and stud, Wesley doesn't really know many stunts. He'll lick butter off a fake wall socket to seem to be electrocuting himself, or stand on the ledge of a window as though contemplating a jump. But otherwise, the admittedly black-humor jokes arise from Wesley's weary, careworn face, aged to decrepitude by a little white makeup around the muzzle, or from his naturally stiff body, seemingly halfway to rigor mortis.

It's a dog's life, working on *Spin City*. Wesley does about ten shows a year, appearing in every second or third episode. He has his own, albeit tiny, dressing room, where he can rehearse a bit and have quiet time in between takes. (A lifelike, custom-made "Rags doll" serves as a stand-in for

his more difficult stunts.) Then it's off to makeup, and maybe to the costumer's to don a tiny pair of pajamas or an elegant doll-sized velvet smoking jacket that matches Carter's. He does

his scene, then gets the only reward that he finds sufficiently motivating—lots and lots of petting and cuddling.

For an actor who does so little, Wesley gets a lion's share of attention. At the end of filming, which is done in front of a live audience at New York City's Chelsea Pier, he gets his own curtain call. The *Spin City* website is never without postings seeking the identity of his breed. And he's done fund-raisers for the Humane Society, schmoozing with such stars as Bernadette Peters, Mary Tyler Moore, and George Segal.

As with most actors whose TV show hits it big, Wesley's a bona-fide celebrity now—when he goes on a walk between takes, people on the street go nuts when they recognize him. But it hasn't gone to Wesley's head. After all is said and done, he has simple needs: a little love, a chance to catch a nap, and if he's feeling hungry, maybe a slice of American cheese, the one doggie treat he really enjoys. Unlike the suicidal Rags, Wesley finds his life well worth living.

With a dab of vegetable-based cosmetics (*opposite*), Wesley goes from looking old to—well, *really* old. The dog, however, gets the last laugh: Before TV, his face won him acclaim as a show dog and catalog model.

Xena STATE TROOPER

Sometimes, it's boring being state trooper Gloria Yarusso's partner —just a lot of sitting around, waiting for speeding cars to whiz by. Sometimes, it's hard on the nerves, getting jostled in the patrol car as it bounces across a median or swings a tight U-turn. But sometimes, it's pure fun —and that's what makes Xena's day. Fun to her is stopping a car and hunting through, around, and under it until she smells something that unmistakably signals "play."

Play, for Xena, means finding substances that some people wrongly use for "play": marijuana, psilocybin mushrooms, cocaine, methamphetamine, and heroin and other opiates. Xena can sniff them out no matter how carefully they've been concealed. She's part of a new wave in drug dogs. Instead of burly German Shepherds, the Minnesota State Patrol has turned to lightweight Belgian Malinois, a breed armed with an incredible sense of smell and an unfailing drive to hunt.

Xena's the most laid-back of the ten Malinois now patrolling Minnesota's roads. But when Trooper Yarusso gives the cue, Xena springs to life. If she smells one of her target odors, she freezes and almost stops breathing, so pure is her focus. Then she bursts into a fury of scratching and barking. Yarusso knows that Xena's found paydirt. Xena only knows that she's won the game, and it's time for her prize: a rousing bout of tug-of-war with the trooper.

● **57** ●

"When we're in the car, Xena likes to lean in from the back seat and lay her head on my shoulder," says Yarusso.

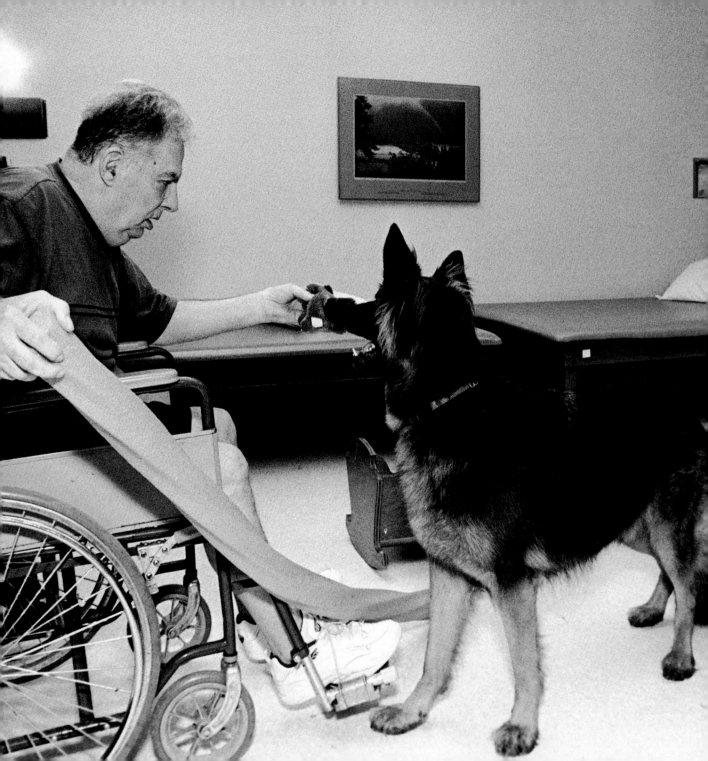

susie & thor PHYSICAL THERAPISTS

The man is struggling to say the words. "Su … sie." His voice is faint. Susie waits on the other side of the room, her big brown eyes glued to his face. Her whole being is focused on him, seemingly as if she is drawing the words from his lips. The man sighs. Parkinson's disease is incurable, has ravaged his ability to speak. … Sometimes it's hard to want to try. Why bother? But Susie is watching, waiting, trained to hold still until the man can produce a full, clear command. She almost looks as though she wants him to do it, wants him to call her. He rallies himself one more time and expels the words, "Susie, fetch this," as he extends a toy. Joyfully, she leaps for the plaything, just as he directed. Man and dog both smile as he slips Susie a treat to reward her for her poise.

Working with therapists to assist Parkinson's patients in rehabilitation is a high-stress occupation, one that 90 percent of all the other dogs on earth can't do, won't do. Waiting calmly while a treat dangles in view, not grabbing it until the person lifts his weakened arm to a certain height or projects his strained voice to a certain volume … patience such as this does not come naturally to a canine. But Susie and her son, Thor, can handle it. Susie is a natural. She's sensitive to emotions; somehow, her patients' struggles seem to resonate with her. Thor sometimes grapples with his assignments, and will just walk away if he gets bored. His shortcom-

holistic healthcare facility for Parkinson's patients, she took Susie in.

It soon became obvious that Susie could do much more than Ouhl first thought, so the center devised an eight-week pilot program to see if dogs could be useful in therapy sessions. Two years later, the experiment has evolved into business as usual. Susie and Thor have four clients at the center whom they assist with speech, physical, and occupational therapies.

It's taxing work for all involved: After about half an hour, the two shepherds are done in and enjoy a rest period before returning to work. But the animals' involvement is amazingly effective. "Patients love the dogs, and try harder with them," Ouhl explains, "especially if we're teaching a dog something new." This spurs the clients on even more, she notes, "because they see the dog try and fail, just like they do."

ings, though, can be used to advantage: A patient has to keep up with him, which can be an effective challenge for someone with a competitive spirit.

The dogs became physical therapists by accident. When Susie's owner, Carol Ouhl, saw that the German Shepherd clearly hated the obedience competitions for which she had been trained, Ouhl searched for something the dog could do. Ouhl knew Susie had a lovable, snuggly nature, so when she saw a notice seeking pets to visit at the Struthers Center, a

Susie and Thor are so good at their job, they seem to predict which way patients Jim Brooks (*p. 58*) and Adrian Lin (*opposite*) will move next. Canine intuition? Not quite: They read the men's eyes.

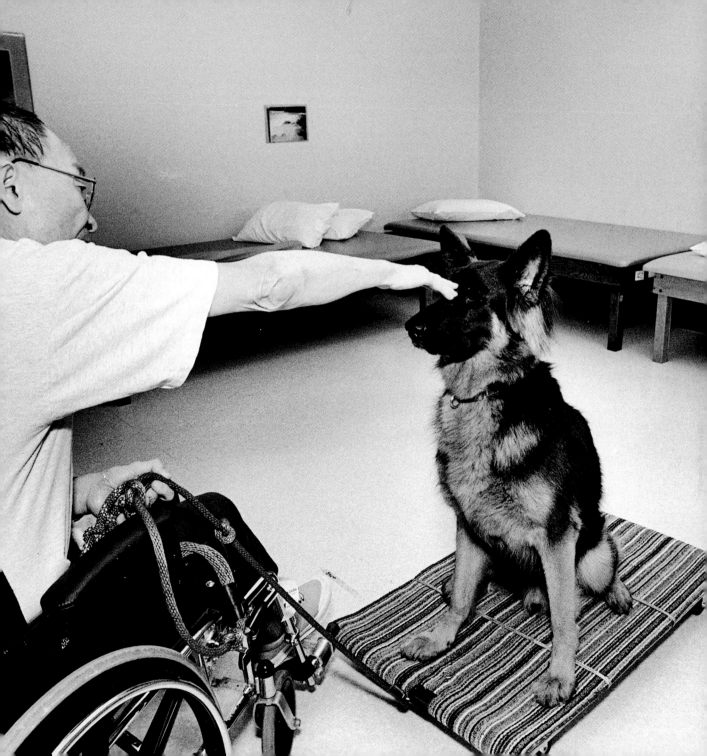

tattie GROUNDSKEEPER

Tattie loves the golf cart, loves rolling over the roughs and fairways past pristine sand traps and shimmering ponds. This hundred-and-seventy-acre stretch of Ellsworth Meadows Golf Club in Hudson, Ohio, is her domain—terrain where no Canada goose dares set its webbed foot. Because if Tattie spies even a single misguided goose in the distance, she starts trembling and squirming.

On course manager Denny Smith's command, and with all the herding instinct of her border collie forebears surging through her, Tattie launches. She'll try a variety of approaches: slowly stalking until the geese nervously take flight, charging right into the lake to frighten them off, or breaking small groups off from a larger flock and driving them away, bunch by bunch. Tattie's good at her job—so good, in fact, that in just six months she convinced four hundred and fifty of the birds who had established residency to find new homes.

Border collies are becoming a popular and humane way to drive brazen Canada geese away from golf courses, parks, office complexes, and school campuses everywhere. Where others have tried gunshots, machines, and screened fences and have failed, the dynamic dogs have succeeded. Smith can't say enough about his four-legged groundskeeper: "She's a highly effective employee. She's done her job so well that now the geese will leave at the sight of a golf cart, whether Tattie's on it or not."

63

Tattie in Maytag-repairman mode: Like the famous advertising scenario, she often has nothing to do now.

lucy ARSON DETECTIVE

The custom-built workshop of a Merrimack, Massachusetts, carpenter was still smoldering when arson inspector Paul Horgan and his black lab, Lucy, arrived at the scene. In the predawn darkness, a fire truck's flashing lights swept across the distraught face of a woman, owner of the unburned home just a few feet away. The carpenter whose shop was destroyed was her estranged husband. Despite a restraining order, he had called his wife at midnight, and she had hung up on him. Two hours later, the workshop was in flames.

Lucy set to work immediately, sniffing through the charred wood and cinders. Suddenly, she sat, looking around expectantly for a handful of kibble. Horgan fed her a treat, then said, "Show me." Lucy put her nose flat to the floor. Horgan took a sample to send to the crime lab, but finding evidence of arson wasn't enough. They had to find the culprit. He and Lucy then went with a search warrant to the house where the carpenter was staying. In his room, Lucy went straight to a new pair of sneakers and sat down. The shoes were confiscated for the lab as well. Then, the suspect watched in amazement as Lucy went out to sniff the interior of his car. She alerted again. The man choked, then blurted a confession. He knew that Lucy had nailed him.

The case of the Merrimack carpenter is one of more than nine hundred fire scenes that Lucy has investigated in her five years as an "accelerant detection canine." She's an arson investigator with a special gift—a keen

nose trained to detect seventeen different ignitable liquids. She has also been blessed with high energy and an obsession to chase things, qualities that led her to be expelled from guide-dog school, but which make her an outstanding arson dog. Through layers of debris that are redolent with smoke and the distracting aroma of melted plastics that smell like some accelerants, Lucy still gets it right more than 90 percent of the time.

"Will work for food" could be Lucy's motto; no doubt it's a large part of her success. That's because she's trained to associate finding the right odor with getting food. Every mouthful of kibble she eats, at home and on the job, comes only from Paul Horgan's hand. This strengthens their bond, and also keeps Lucy's skills at their peak, because even during down time she and Horgan are training, methodically building Lucy's detection abilities through thousands of repetitions.

With the exception of her feeding routine, Lucy lives the normal life of a pet in the Horgan family, playing, going for walks, lolling about as her energy wanes with age. After five years on the force, Lucy is a veteran now, and is just a year away from retirement. Then, she'll be allowed to eat what she wants, to beg from the table, to never sniff another training target. In fact, Horgan says, "the first day she retires, I'm getting that dog a bowl."

Lucy is one of only two hundred arson detection canines in the United States; she and her gifted nose are on call night and day. Horgan makes sure she's protected by first checking the scene himself for spilled chemicals or broken glass.

sarah, dottie, joe & claire

Sarah likes hers crunchy and crisp. Joe likes his soft and sweet. Dottie likes hers flavorful and savory. Claire likes any of it, any time, any place. As the dogs of the Three Dog Bakery, a chain of doggie treat boutiques, these hard-working hounds are the first line of quality control. They spend all day at the main bakery in Kansas City, Missouri, tasting the Pupcakes and the Bark-B-Que Ribs and the Great Danish just as

fast as they come off the line. No product can be offered to the public until these dogs have given their slurp of approval.

Sarah, a twelve-year-old black lab, is the only one left of the original three dogs. She's the grand matriarch. Joe, a Great Dane, was born deaf, and rescued by bak-

ery owner Dan Dye. Joe's just a year old, but he's already proven to have a discerning palate. Dottie, a little beagle-dalmatian mix, is the friendliest, wiggliest, snuggliest dog of the three. They all have the ability to distinguish tasty treats from not-so-tasty treats, a quality not matched by their "country cousin," Claire. An albino Great Dane, Claire was also born deaf; she grew up hungry on the streets and was abused by people along the way. If she could, this fourth and much-loved member of the Three Dog Bakery, thrilled to be an auxiliary taste tester, would no doubt tell you that now, things just couldn't be any sweeter.

Sarah licks her chops (*above*), while Dottie and Joe feast on Three Dog Bakery's signature carob chip cake.

Dan Dye and Mark Beckloff (*right*) developed their doggie treats with guidance from veterinarians and breeders, along with many a discriminating dog palate.

Joe (*left*) and his cohorts (*p. 68*)—including lookalike Claire—stand outside the bakery, luring customers with their puppy-dog eyes.

lassie

Lassie. For baby boomers, that word brings back memories of Sunday evenings spent glued to the TV set, watching the beautiful collie with the courageous spirit. It compels them to race to wherever the dog might be making an appearance, so they can touch the soft coat, hear the piercing bark that still seems to say, "Timmy's in trouble—come on!"

Today, Lassie's still hot enough to have a TV series on Animal Planet, sell a million copies of the latest Lassie movie. Folks can't resist this eighth Lassie, the great-great-great-great-great grandchild of the original dog who began the phenomenon in 1943 with *Lassie Come Home*. Like that dog and every other Lassie since, this collie is a male. In addition, they've all been trained by a member of the Weatherwax

family—Bob Weatherwax now carries on the legacy of his father Rudd, who also trained Toto from *The Wizard of Oz*.

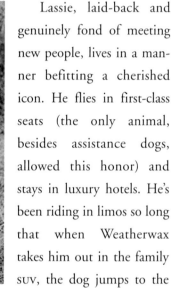

Lassie, laid-back and genuinely fond of meeting new people, lives in a manner befitting a cherished icon. He flies in first-class seats (the only animal, besides assistance dogs, allowed this honor) and stays in luxury hotels. He's been riding in limos so long that when Weatherwax takes him out in the family SUV, the dog jumps to the very back seat as if Bob were his chauffeur.

But this Lassie's getting gray around the muzzle. Soon, he'll enjoy more time relaxing around the Weatherwax house, and his son, Laddie, will assume the task of warming the hearts of the middle-aged. Laddie, then, will be Lassie, the collie of collies.

Lassie has his own bedroom in Weatherwax's home, where a replica of Lassie's Hollywood Walk of Fame star hangs.

scruffy CHAPLAIN

"Good morning," Kay Miller announced cheerfully as she entered the hospital room. "I thought you might like a visit." The man lifted his head and waved weakly at the volunteer chaplain and Scruffy, her mixed-breed dog. Miller knew that the man's wife had died and been buried while he was in the hospital. She knew that he was refusing to mourn, or even to talk about his wife. Scruffy knew only that the man was sad and wanted to pet her.

As he ran his fingers through her silken coat, the man began talking to Scruffy, almost as if Miller wasn't there. First, he talked about his dog, then about how his wife used to play with the animal. Then he started telling Scruffy about his wife's death, and he began to cry. Scruffy stayed by his side, nuzzling him lightly from time to time. But once the man began telling her about his plans for killing himself once he got out of the hospital, Scruffy stiffened. She moved away just out of his reach, and would not return, no matter how he coaxed. Finally, the man said, "You're right, I shouldn't do this. My grandkids need me." And with that, Scruffy walked right back over and let him stroke her again as he considered plans for his new life.

As a pastoral care dog, Scruffy helps Miller minister to people in crisis. The mutt's uncanny ability to sense emotions makes her ideal for the field of hospital chaplaincy. "Scruffy helps open doors,"

● 75 ●

explains Miller. "Until that man could talk with her about his pain, his profound spiritual needs couldn't be addressed. Once he opened up, then we could talk about what it means to take your own life, and how that didn't fit into his spiritual framework."

Scruffy's remarkable aid doesn't stop there. When Miller was in a car accident in 1995, her family sent Scruffy to be trained as a service dog, and now the canine knows what to do when Miller has seizures. Scruffy is also a trained therapy dog, assisting physical, occupational, and speech therapists at St. Mark's Hospital in Salt Lake City.

For her efforts, Scruffy was acknowledged in 1999 by the Delta Society (a national licensing organization for therapy animals) as one of the top three therapy dogs in the United States.

Miller and Scruffy do most of their chaplain work at St. Mark's. But they'll also dispatch to disaster centers, as they did in 1999 when a tornado ripped through the city. The twister had flipped a car carrying two sisters; one of the women was critically injured. The other woman, seared by the image of her bleeding sibling, poured out her heart to the dog. "She had a horrible, gruesome story to tell," Miller says. "I was there, but she told it to Scruffy."

More than a sympathetic ear: Something about Scruffy makes people like Brian Lewis (*previous page*) and Fern Rothe (*opposite*) open up and share their feelings.

franklin POLITICAL CONSULTANT

No one steals the thunder from Jesse Ventura. No one, that is, except his no-nonsense, crowd-pleasing English bulldog. Like his master, this canine knows how to dominate the limelight and is no stranger to career detours.

His name was recently changed to "The Bulldog Formerly Known as Franklin," a fitting moniker for a dog from the same state as The Artist Formerly Known as Prince and owned by a governor formerly known as a pro wrestler. "In Minnesota," Ventura jokes, "when you get famous, you have to change your name."

It's the third such switch for the four-footed Ventura, who was born under the pedigree title of Sir Frances Bacon. When Jesse and Terry Ventura first adopted him six years ago and brought him to their horse ranch, they simply called him Franklin. The plucky dog quickly showed he was a born leader, barking orders to the American Saddlebreds he found in the barn like a bona-fide wrangler. Even though his much larger charges would occasional kick him in the head, nothing kept Franklin down for long, not when there was security detail to attend to or trail rides to lead.

When the political upset of the century sent Franklin's master to the Minnesota capitol, Franklin assumed his new duties at the governor's mansion with the same panache and bravado that he's always exhibited. With no horses to be found, Franklin spotted the next best thing and began herding the tour groups that frequently come through the official residence.

When he is not in the public eye, The Bulldog Formerly Known as Franklin assists Governor Ventura as a political consultant, specializing in motivational techniques. As the state's only Reform Party elected official, the governor likes to call the dog in to break up impasses between Republican and Democratic legislators. "He's a great mediator," says the Governor. "He gives legislators only so much time to settle their dispute before it's time to go outside to chase squirrels," and, presumably, time for the officials to move to the next order of business.

Franklin guides visitors throughout the grand reception areas, stopping now and then at a particularly sunny spot where he likes to nap. He manages to get in all photo shoots, official or otherwise, and even upstages the models during charity fashion shows—he's fond of ambling down the runway during the final curtain call. All of these antics have made him so popular ("the heartthrob of all who come to the governor's mansion," says Ventura) that he now has his own press secretary, not to mention the longer, and cooler, name.

Despite his huge following, this "pol" manages to keep all four paws firmly on the ground, and still enjoys his favorite "off-duty" pursuits: chasing bubbles, swinging from trees, and taking quick dips in the formal water gardens. For the littlest Ventura in the governor's mansion, it's anything but politics as usual.

One determined dog: When the Ventura family vacations, it's not unusual for Franklin to try his paw at windsurfing.

ginny

Philip Gonzalez had owned Ginny only three days when the cat business started. Early one morning, while walking the schnauzer-husky mix past a vacant lot, Gonzalez lost his grip on Ginny's leash when she charged a cat. He expected to hear hisses and growls, but the cat fearlessly ran up to Ginny, and in minutes, the two were friends.

As months passed, Ginny unearthed more strays, most of them down on their luck—deaf cats, cats with brain damage, abandoned kittens. Gonzalez soon began bringing a cat carrier on their walks around his Long Beach, N.Y., neighborhood, and he watched in amazement as the little gray dog convinced stray after skittish stray to climb inside. Gonzalez took each cat to a veterinarian to have it treated, neutered, and if possible, adopted. If a cat was too wild to find a home, the vet notched one ear so it could be identified, and Gonzalez set it free. Today—546 rescues later—no one knows why cats respond to Ginny, but her work continues to win recognition. She was even named "Cat of the Year" by the Westchester Feline Club.

But Ginny's greatest rescue is probably her first: She rescued a lost human. Phil Gonzalez had become disabled after an accident on the job. Depressed and unmotivated, he almost never left his apartment. Then, a friend suggested he get a dog, so Gonzalez went down to the animal shelter. There he rescued Ginny. Or maybe it was the other way around.

$\cdot$ **83** $\cdot$

Ginny and Gonzalez—who, before the cat rescues began, wasn't even a "cat person"—share their tiny apartment with an ever-changing cast of grateful felines.

belle   FARMHAND

It's 5 A.M., time to do the chores. Dave Zimmerman and his golden retriever Belle roll out quickly. Dave rolls literally—a paraplegic, he's been in a wheelchair since his motorcycle was hit by a car in 1986. Belle is Dave's service dog. As his hired hand, she helps him keep the farm working, rain or shine. After breakfast, Belle brings Dave his shoes, opens the door and closes it behind them, then hops into the cab of an ATV with him and heads for the hog shed half a mile down the road.

There, Belle helps Dave clean the pig pens by bringing him scrapers and the hose, and opening and closing the shed doors. If Dave drops his tools, or needs something fetched, Belle's got it. For a reward, she gets to play with her tennis ball—when Dave tosses it, Belle races after it so fast that she tumbles head over heels to stop when she catches up. An independent, self-directed worker, Belle dislikes wearing her harness, preferring to roam and play freely when Dave doesn't need her help. Still, she'll do almost anything he asks, although she's not wild about riding on the bumpy snowplow or tractor.

Belle is a great American farm dog, but she became one only because in 1994 Dave entered a "Great American Farm Dog" contest. Sponsored by *Successful Farming* magazine and Rhone Poulenc Herbicide, the competition promised a dog to anyone who could best explain why his or her farm needed one.

Dave wrote a lengthy description of his

accident, his disability, his life as the owner of a small family farm in Minnesota, and how a dog could help him carry on. Of the 429 entries the magazine received, Dave's was the most compelling.

Belle was his grand prize, selected and trained by Independence Dogs in Pennsylvania to be a service dog. The agency had never trained a dog for farmwork before, so there were lots of phone calls to the Zimmermans as Belle began to learn the tasks she would have to perform. She even spent time at the University of Delaware's swine farm to get used to working with hogs.

Finally, almost two years after Dave wrote his essay, Belle arrived. She fit right in with Dave, with his wife and two kids, with his brothers and parents (who own neighboring farms), even with the hogs. Her upbeat yet mellow personality makes her welcome wherever Dave goes, whether it's to his part-time desk job in a neighbor-

ing town, or to Walt Disney World for a family vacation. "After my accident, I was taught to do everything for myself," says Dave, "so it took me a while to integrate her into my life while still maximizing my ability to be independent. But she's made my life so much easier, so much more fulfilling."

Belle brings a hammer to Dave (*opposite*). The talented retriever can pick up an object as small as a credit card, or as cumbersome as a rake. She's up for any task, but scoots out of reach if Dave tries to harness her.

gidget ADVERTISING SPOKESPERSON

Those bat-like ears. Those doe-like eyes. That insouciant attitude. It's got to be Gidget, the Taco Bell spokesdog who has everyone swooning, "*Yo quiero la Chihuahua.*" Since her debut in the fast-food eatery's advertising campaign in 1997, the diminutive dog has seen the chain's sales—and her own star—soar. *People* magazine listed Gidget as one of its 25 Most Intriguing People that year, and *Entertainment Weekly* put her on its "It List." Bidding wars erupted on the Internet for stuffed Chihuahua toys, and the demand for real Chihuahua puppies grew until breeders couldn't keep up.

Why the frenzy? It's partly Gidget's natural appeal, and it's partly the role she plays. Although Gidget is a female, her character in the commercials is a sexy, hip *chico*, or male, dog. "He"

runs, sits, stays, tilts his head, and oozes star quality, all at the bidding of trainer Sue Chipperton. A computer provides animation for Gidget's eyebrows and lips, while comic Carlos Alazraqui gives the dog a voice. But even without technical tweaking, "Gidget's a better actor than some of the humans," notes creative director Chuck Bennett of TBWA Chiat/Day, the agency behind the ads. "She certainly understands her motivation better"—steak and chicken chunks dangled just out of camera range.

• 89 •

¡Yo Quiero Taco Bell!

Gidget, whose prior screen credits include Robert DeNiro's *The Fan*, learned how to jump on top of taxicabs and run on a treadmill for her Taco Bell spots.

bosco BOWLING PIN CHASER

Neffer's bowling alley thunders with the sounds of rolling balls and falling pins, shouting winners and groaning losers who miss the spare. Then, amid the din, a cry rings out: "Pin in the gutter!" Right away, a chocolate lab races from behind the control desk. Then, daintily, he minces down the gutter to an abandoned pin resting out of reach of the automated rake. He seizes it in his mouth and hustles back to the control desk, where he drops it and looks around for his treat.

It's just another day on the job for Bosco, the pin chaser. He's been retrieving errant pins since he was a pup. Back then, Steve Neff—owner of the Homosassa Springs, Florida, alley and of Bosco—wouldn't let the dog budge past the foul line for fear he'd track oil from the shiny lanes across the rest of the floors. Instead, Bosco watched and Neff fetched pins. One day, Neff thought, "This is pretty stupid. The dog can do this." So, beginning with a plastic pin and a pocket full of cookies, he taught Bosco first to get his front paws in the gutter, then to add the back paws, and within two weeks, Bosco was ready to go to work.

Fast forward three years. Bosco is a pro—so much a pro that he accompanies Neff on the Senior Pro Bowlers Tour, chases pins in every alley they visit, and gets his picture included in every program. When Bosco was named the tour's official mascot in 1999, he may have sent a little luck rolling his master's way: Three months later, Neff won the national title.

Bosco, who's become something of a media darling, inspires Steve Neff's friends to kid the newly crowned senior champion: "If you keep bowling so well," said one, "you might be as famous as your dog someday."

Above: "Step in the gutter, not on the lanes" is the rule for this canine pin chaser. He almost always obeys: The one notable exception came when ESPN2 was airing Neff's Brunswick Senior Pro victory, and Bosco—a little too excited, perhaps—cheated the last few feet. Sure enough, all four paws went flying, banana-peel style.

For more information

Nicky, Ginny, Wheely Willy, Goldie, all four of the Three Dog Bakery canines, and all of the Amazing Mongrels: The special talents and unqualified devotion of these working dogs would never have been discovered had the animals not been adopted from shelters and other rescue groups. The following organizations can direct you to groups in your area that shelter and find homes for strays, or otherwise dedicate their efforts to animal issues and to improving the relationship between animals and humans.

THE HUMANE SOCIETY OF THE UNITED STATES
and THE HUMANE SOCIETY INTERNATIONAL
2100 L Street, N.W.
Washington, DC 20037
www.hsus.org
www.animalchannel.org

AMERICAN SOCIETY FOR THE PREVENTION
OF CRUELTY TO ANIMALS (ASPCA)
424 East 92nd Street
New York, NY 10128-6804
(212) 876-7700
www.aspca.org

THE ARK TRUST, INC.
P.O. Box 8191
Universal City, CA 91618-8191
(818) 501-2ARK
Genesis@arktrust.org
www.arktrust.org
This national, nonprofit animal-protection organization is devoted to raising public awareness about animal issues.

Through programs such as the annual Genesis Awards (past honorees include Jane Goodall and Paul McCartney), it promotes positive coverage of animal-welfare topics by the media.

ANIMAL ALLIANCE OF CANADA
221 Broadview Avenue
Suite 101
Toronto, Ontario, Canada M4M 2G3
(416) 462-9541
www.animalalliance.ca
This organization focuses on local, national, and international issues concerning the respectful treatment of animals. Among its chief interests are endangered and protected species, and pet overpopulation.

THE BLUE CROSS
Main Street
Rye, East Sussex, England TN316LP
www.thebluecross.org.uk
Britain's Blue Cross organization works in the areas of pet adoption, animal hospitals and clinics, equine welfare, and more.

THE DELTA SOCIETY

289 Perimeter Road East
Renton, WA 98055-1329
(800) 869-6898
info@deltasociety.org
www.deltasociety.org
This group promotes the role of animals in human health through such programs as Animal-Assisted Therapy Services (improving health in ill people) and the National Service Dog Center (providing independence for disabled people).

CANINE COMPANIONS FOR INDEPENDENCE

P.O. Box 446
Santa Rosa, CA 95402-0446
(800) 572-BARK
www.caninecompanions.org
This nonprofit association provides disabled people with trained service, hearing, and social dogs, and provides ongoing support to the team after placement.

INDEPENDENCE DOGS

146 Stateline Road
Chadds Ford, PA 19317
(610) 358-2723
Independence Dogs provides highly trained service dogs for children and adults with mobility impairments.

GUIDE DOGS FOR THE BLIND

P.O. Box 151200
San Rafael, CA 94915-1200
(800) 295-4050
www.guidedogs.com
This organization provides guide dogs and training in their use to visually impaired people in the United States and Canada.

INTERMOUNTAIN THERAPY ANIMALS

2035 South 1300 East
Salt Lake City, UT 84105
(877) 485-1121
This group offers animal-assisted aid in psychotherapy, special education, and physical, occupational, and speech therapies.

WIND RIVER BEAR INSTITUTE

P.O. Box 307
Heber City, UT 84032
(435) 654-6644
windriver@shadowlink.net
www.beardogs.com
The Institute's "Partners in Life" program works to reduce conflicts between humans and bears by using Karelian bear dogs to teach bears to behave in a manner that does not put them at odds with people, and to educate humans about respecting bear behavior.

THE GINNY FUND

470 East Broadway
Apartment C1
Long Beach, NY 11561
Through his nonprofit fund, Philip Gonzalez uses contributions to feed, house, place, and obtain medical care for the hundreds of cats found by his dog, Ginny.

DOG SCOUTS OF AMERICA

5068 Nestel Road East
St. Helen, MI 48656
(517) 389-2000
dogscouts@aol.com
www.dogscouts.com
Held several times each year in Michigan, Dog Scouts camp brings together canines and their owners for training in water safety and rescue, drug detection, scent tracking, hiking, and other activities that encourage owners to spend more time outdoors with their dogs, and that teach the canines how to be of more assistance in return.

NATIONAL ASSOCIATION FOR SEARCH AND RESCUE

4500 Southgate Place, Suite 100
Chantilly, VA 20151-1714
(703) 222-6277
www.nasar.org
info@nasar.org
The nonprofit NASAR assists both paid personnel and volunteers working in search and rescue, disaster aid, and emergency medicine.

To Ruffy and Stogie, the world's best publicity hounds—C.N.
To my greyhounds, Lani and Moxie—retired and loving it.—K.C.
For John and Charlie—K.L.

DISCOVERY COMMUNICATIONS, INC.

John S. Hendricks
Founder, Chairman, and Chief Executive Officer

Judith A. McHale
President and Chief Operating Officer

Michela English
President
Discovery Enterprises Worldwide

Judy L. Harris
Senior Vice President, Consumer Products
Discovery Enterprises Worldwide

DISCOVERY CHANNEL PUBLISHING

Natalie Chapman
Vice President, Publishing

Rita Thievon Mullin
Editorial Director

Mary Kalamaras
Senior Editor

Maria Mihalik Higgins
Editor

Michael Hentges
Art Director

Heather Quinlan
Editorial Coordinator

Christine Alvarez
Business Development

Discovery Communications, Inc., produces high-quality television programming, interactive media, books, films, and consumer products. Discovery Networks, a division of Discovery Communications, Inc., operates and manages the Discovery Channel, TLC, Animal Planet, Travel Channel, and the Discovery Health Channel.

Copyright ©2000 by Discovery Communications, Inc. All rights reserved under International and Pan-American Copyright Conventions. Published in the United States by Discovery Books, an imprint of Random House, Inc., New York, and simultaneously in Canada by Random House of Canada Limited, Toronto.

Discovery Books and the Discovery Books colophon are trademarks of Discovery Communications, Inc.

No part of this book may be reproduced in any form or by any electronic or mechanical means, including information storage and retrieval devices or systems, without prior written permission from the publisher, except that brief passages may be quoted for reviews.

Book and cover design: Lisa Vaughn, Two of Cups Studio
Additional production thanks to John Spaulding.

Library of Congress Cataloging-in-Publication data is available.
ISBN 1-56331-843-1 (hardcover)

Discovery Communications website address: www.discovery.com
Random House website address: www.atrandom.com

Printed in China on acid-free paper
10 9 8 7 6 5 4 3 2 1
First Edition

COLLEEN NEEDLES is an award-winning television journalist and president of Tremendous! Entertainment, Inc. She is the creator of the television series *K-9 to 5*, which appears on the Animal Planet network and is the inspiration behind this book. Colleen lives in Minneapolis with her husband, three children, and two dogs.

KIT CARLSON is a science and nature writer, author of *Bringing Up Baby: Wild Animal Families* and co-author of *The Leopard Son*. She lives with two rescued racing greyhounds, two half-grown children, and a patient husband.

KIM LEVIN is a New York-based photographer and owner of Bark & Smile Pet Portraits®. She is the author of *Why We Love Dogs* and *Why We Really Love Dogs*.

Additional photo credits: Batty, pp. 12 and 14, Madeline de Sinety. Tess, p. 26, Scott Sine; p. 27, Wind River Bear Institute; p. 28, Gary Martin; p. 29, Lonnie Raymond. Gidget, p. 88, Vern Evans; p. 99, Michael Rupert.